Budapest

Domokos Varga

Budapest

315 Colour Photographs

Corvina

1. *View of Budapest*
2–4. *Two river banks, but one city*

Buda and Pest

Many cities grace the banks of the Rhine, and as many lie along the Volga. But the Danube is the only river in Europe whose waters run through eight countries and wash the stones of three capitals. Of the three Danubian capitals, Budapest enjoys a central location. From Vienna, the river flows on and through it before continuing its course towards Belgrade. Both Vienna and Belgrade are predominantly right-bank cities. It is on the right bank of the Danube that their present-day centres have developed in the course of the centuries.

But what about Budapest?

The river that flows through this city divides it into two parts: Buda and Pest. If we trace the pulse of the city with due attention, we shall observe that its left bank appears to throb more intensely to make the centre of Pest the heart of the capital.

6

In Vienna, too, the Danube cuts the city in two, but only because the growing city has expanded beyond the river.

In Budapest, on the other hand, two separate cities have developed on the two banks, competing with each other and yet joined by countless ties.

Here, the Danube is much wider than in Vienna. Formerly, all river transport had to be suspended in winter, an interruption which lasted for weeks, sometimes months. Yet through the centuries, Pest was nevertheless kept alive mainly by the fact that Buda was there on the opposite bank, while Buda owed its animation to the existence of Pest across the river. More precisely, both cities owed their prosperity to the fact that since ancient times, they have represented the most convenient place for crossing the middle reaches of the Danube.

The Hungarian Plain, the famous *puszta,* stretches right up to the boundaries of Pest, which is built on the western edge of this spacious prairie. But Buda, on the right bank, is situated on the eastern border of forest-clad

7

hills. Here, merchants arriving from various directions always found buyers for their money, gold or silver.

Lying on the plain, Pest was enabled to grow into a large city first of all by the exertions of its own craftsmen and merchants. Buda could boast a special feature: the Castle Hill rising above the Danube. From the thirteenth century on, all the kings of Hungary in the late Middle Ages resided upon the long plateau of this hilly land, and thus Buda became the centre of the government of the country.

The first permanent bridge over the Danube, the Chain Bridge, was constructed between the twin cities in the 1840s. It was only around this time that the thought of uniting Buda and Pest to form the capital of Hungary, then embarked on the road of modern development, was first seriously suggested. But the name to be given to the united city was a matter that required lengthy consideration. Some preferred to call it Pest-Buda, even before the two places had been officially united. Others referred to it as Buda-Pest. Eventually, the new city was called Budapest.

The official unification of Pest and Buda took place in 1872. The small territory of Óbuda (Old Buda), situated north of Buda, was also attached to the city. Together the three geographical units formed Budapest, the capital of Hungary. The new capital enjoyed equal rights with Vienna, for in 1867 Hungary acquired the rank of co-dominion with Austria within the Habsburg Empire.

Today, Budapest has six major bridges instead of one, plus one railway bridge to the north and another to the south of the city. A subway (the Metro) passes under the Danube. However, anyone heading for the opposite bank is still said to be going to "Buda" or "Pest" respectively. In the same way, it is natural for people to say "I live in Buda," or "I work in Pest". As long as Budapest exists, Buda and Pest will survive ineradicably under their old, respective names.

Perspectives

No city in the world looks equally beautiful from every angle. Thus, the particular vantage point from which one views Budapest is not irrelevant. The briefest initial exploration will reveal quite a number of unsightly houses and districts. However, thanks to the city's many well-favoured aspects, its lovely parts are even more easily discovered.

It is sufficient to halt anywhere along the Pest bank of the Danube and look across at the rows of houses, squares, churches and hills on the opposite side. Bare rocks, gardens, parks, houses of different sizes, towers, bastions and castle walls present a variegated view. But it is perhaps even better not to pause at any one point, for the scene varies constantly as we walk along the bank, giving particular appeal to the magnificent view unfolding before us. Perhaps the best is to board a river-cruise boat and enjoy the sight of both Buda and Pest simultaneously along the full length of their banks.

Viewed from the Buda side of the river, the perspective is also fascinating, especially from the top of Gellért Hill and Castle Hill. These elevations rise so abruptly over the river that river craft seem to float at their feet, and the close-packed buildings of Pest appear to be only an arm's length away.

When one has had one's fill of the view of Pest, the Danube, the islands, bridges and boats from the nearby hilltops, one can easily find a new perspective. By turning one's back on the view, after a few minutes' walk the semicircle of the more distant hills of Óbuda opens in the opposite direction, where thou-

10

sands of family houses have been built into the tree-clad hillsides. Here and there some larger apartment blocks appear among them, but fortunately, these are not numerous enough as yet to spoil the unified effect of the vast landscape. Its main outlines are drawn not by human hand but by nature herself. The houses do not markedly disrupt the ridges of the hills, nor is the effect of the high places reduced by skyscrapers. Both these circumstances enhance the charm of the view.

The highest peak to be seen is János-hegy. This 528 metres high forested area is situated within the boundaries of Budapest. It is topped by a look-out tower with a terrace which commands a circular view which is unique in the capital. Eastwards, Budapest stretches out far below, while to the north, south and west the mountainous region of Buda undulates in the hazy distance.

Neither Buda, nor Pest

The Danube, its islands, boats and bridges belong neither to Buda nor to Pest.

The title of the famous "Blue Danube" waltz is deceptive. The river is not blue, not even in Vienna, and still less in Budapest. However, the camera does not believe the human eye, and always depicts the greenish-grey river in more vivid hues.

The Danube does not owe its colour to the pollution that is the byproduct of modernization. It is natural to it, and is probably produced by the quantity of fine grains of sand floating in the water. Every river carries large quantities of alluvial material: stones, pebbles, sand and silt, but where its current slackens, it always deposits part of these. The river at Budapest was suitable for such deposits in two particularly large areas. North of the city, the Danube spreads beyond its narrow bed to form the Danube Bend at Visegrád, below which it tries to rid itself of part of its burden by creating Szentendre Island, which stretches for over 30 km as far as Budapest. This is followed by a number of smaller islands within the area of the capital. The next 5 or 6 km of the river has no islands, since the Danube cuts the city centre in two.

12–13. *On and above the river*
14. *Towards Margaret Island*
15. *Here the boats must fight the tide*
16. *Waiting for a boat*

Then at its lower reaches, it forms the 50 km long Csepel Island.

The ferry between Buda and Pest once attracted itinerant merchants, cattle drovers and travellers because here they could cross directly from one bank to the other, whereas if they travelled through the islanded reaches, they would have had to cross two branches of the river.

True, ferry-men here had to cope with a much stronger current. Castle Hill and Gellért Hill, both rising on the Buda bank, narrow the river bed. They apply spurs to its flank, like a rider urging his steed to a gallop.

This explains why there are no islands in this section of the river. The first bridge was also built at this point, because it could accommodate the shortest span. After Szentendre, Margaret Island is the most beautiful and the best known among the smaller Danube islands. Its southern tip extends right into the heart of the city. Earlier it was eroded by the strong current of the Danube. Above its northern tip, closer to Pest, there once stood an islet called Fürdő Sziget (Bathing Island) with several thermal springs; however, it was gradually washed away by the river. But Margaret Island was large enough to survive. What the river washed away from its upper

17. *Margaret Island*
18. *Entrance to the Island*

end, it always deposited lower down. Thus, the island kept "swimming" downward about 2 cm a year, until it was fixed in place with bridges; then both its flanks were faced with stone slabs to set it at rest.

Today, the island is a quiet and restful retreat in the busy city. It forms, in effect, one huge park with many old trees and miriads of flowers. Its bushes are lovers' hideaways, its lawns playgrounds; old people rest on its benches. Private cars are banned, except for vehicles bound fòr the hotels situated at the northern end of the island, which can be approached over Árpád Bridge.

When the inhabitants of Budapest say to each

19–23. *There's not another haven like it in the bustling capital*

other "Let's go to the Island," or "Let's meet tomorrow on the Island," they always mean Margaret Island. For them, it is *the* island, the one and only island of the capital.

There are bathing facilities, tennis courts, an open-air theatre and cinema, an old and a new thermal hotel, restaurants, a small zoo, all of which fortunately do not occupy too much space on the more than 2 km long island. Plenty of room remains for the park. The park is the most important feature of the island. Strict building regulations ensure its preservation as the most tranquil and most highly frequented green area within Budapest.

24. *The thermal lake*
25. *The former church of the Premonstratensians*
26–29. *Joys on the island and by the riverside*

The park is much more than a public garden; it carries many historic associations. In the Middle Ages it was the site of a Dominican convent in which the daughter of King Béla IV (1235–1270) took the veil. After the great Mongolian devastation in 1241–1242, this thirteenth-century Hungarian king, who is also called "the builder of the nation," built a castle for himself in Buda. The Princess, whose name was Margaret, lived out her brief, ascetic life in such piety, and performed so many good deeds attended by divine miracles, that she was beatified and later canonized by the Church. The island is named in honour of her memory. Earlier, it was called the Isle of Hares. The ruins of the ancient Dominican convent and church are still extant.

Near the Dominican convent stood the church of the Premonstratensian friars. Part of its twelfth-century foundations and walls have survived. The church was reconstructed in the Romanesque style in the 1930s. In the centre of the island, next to the Rose Garden, stand the ruins of a fourteenth-century Franciscan church.

Bridges. Boats. Harbours. A floating restaurant on a decommissioned boat. Here and there, riverside anglers grown stiff from im-

The bridges spanning the river

Looked at with the eyes of a local inhabitant, the bridges are part of the familiar view of Budapest. It is as if they had joined the two banks of the river since times immemorial, and that nothing could destroy either their slender bodies or their massive stone pillars. Yet there are witnesses aplenty who had seen the bridges destroyed by expertly placed demolition charges in the winter of 1944–1945. They were destroyed because Hitler had

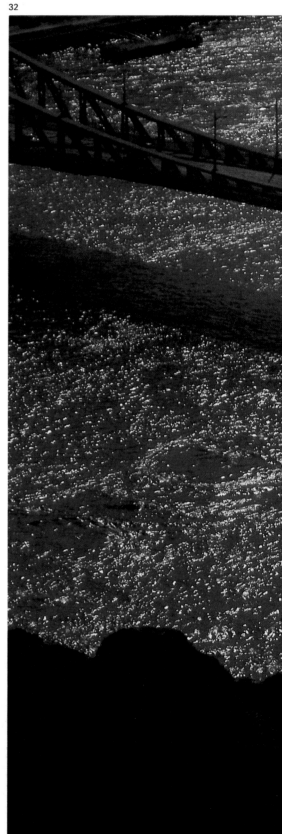

mobility scrutinize the surface of the river with endless patience for a catch. Obliviously, young couples kiss; schoolboys study; children play with pebbles on the steps leading down to the water's edge.

But here again, it is the city with its variety of buildings that attracts our attention. The two banks, Pest and Buda. Or Buda and Pest.

30. *Liberty Bridge with the* turul *birds*
31. *By the river, you can always find a fisherman or two with infinite patience*
32. *As if it had been rising above the river since time immemorial...*

ordered the German troops then surrounded in Budapest to hold out to the last against the besieging Soviet army. That the Germans were driven from Pest to more easily defensible Buda ensured the ruin of the Danube bridges.

True, it ensured their own ruin as well. The ruin of those who blew up the bridges, who died in obedience to orders, and who were responsible for the deaths of so many thousands of hungry old women and children.

The dead are buried, but the bridges stand again, showing none of the signs of the earlier destruction.

Yes, they seem to have spanned the river since time immemorial. From north to south, they are: the Árpád Bridge, Margaret Bridge, the Chain Bridge, Elizabeth Bridge, Liberty (Szabadság) Bridge and Petőfi Bridge. Budapest is unimaginable without them.

The bridges are indispensable; in fact, we could do with more. For the people of Budapest, they not only provide faster transport and communication between the city and the

country; they belong to the city's scape. This applies especially to Margaret Bridge resting upon the southern part of Margaret Island, and, the Chain Bridge and Liberty Bridge. Margaret Bridge, which is over a hundred years old, spans the river in a rather unusual V-form, for this was the only solution permitting the construction of a third abutment leading onto the island.

Except for being somewhat wider, today's Chain Bridge is an exact replica of the original bridge built in the 1840s. It appears to continue into the tunnel running under Castle Hill. According to the story told to credulous children, the bridge is pushed into the tunnel at night, and when it is raining.

Many humorous stories abound about this oldest permanent bridge of Budapest. One of them comes from the times when the Hun-

33. *The arch of Elizabeth Bridge on the Pest side of the river*
34. *The axis of Margaret Bridge is interrupted at the southern tip of Margaret Island*
35. *An allegorical being guards the water from each pillar*

garian nobility was still discussing its possible construction. Was the bridge needed or not? Those who were for building it tried to canvas for as many supporters of the project as possible. But an old nobleman whom they tried to persuade to vote in favour of it, urging him how nice it would be to cross the river safely even in the dead of winter, merely waved his hand sadly, and said with wise resignation: "What is the good of it for the little time I have left?"

The southern neighbour of the Chain Bridge, the Elizabeth Bridge, was built – in its original form, at least – at the turn of the century.

36. *From the Chain Bridge the road leads into the tunnel under Castle Hill*
37. *The stone lions of the Chain Bridge*
38–40. *Elizabeth Bridge,*
the city's most graceful bridge

41–42. *István Széchenyi (1791–1860)*
initiated the construction of
the first permanent bridge.
The Chain Bridge recalls his memory
43–44. *For the people of Budapest, the bridges*
are more than "works of art" . . .

42

It came to be regarded as the finest bridge in Budapest. But the one now replacing the original is perhaps even lighter and more graceful than the pre-war structure, and appears to float above the river.

South of Elizabeth Bridge stood the bridge named after Francis Joseph, the Habsburg Emperor and one-time King of Hungary. It was reconstructed in 1946 in almost the same form as before, but its name was changed to Liberty (Szabadság) Bridge. Thus it evokes the spirit of the end of the century, while its name is associated with the post-war years.

Hills and thermal springs

One may ask why such a long stretch of the Danube flows almost directly north to south, and why it flows through Budapest in the

45. *Bridges over the Danube*

same direction. According to geologists, a characteristic fault-line in the earth's crust determined the course of the river. The geological layers west of this line became slightly more raised, while those east of it sank somewhat.

It appears that the course of the Danube cuts off the hills of Buda from the territory on its eastern bank. It is enough to look at the barren rocks of Gellért Hill to understand the natural forces that must have been active here in earlier times. The slope of Castle Hill overlooking the river is also steep enough to bring to mind the former movements of the earth's crust in this region.

Buda owes its hilly aspect to these early earth tremors, as does the flat land of Pest which became filled with river ballast, sand and mud. A sunken hilly region, the counterpart and direct continuation of the Buda hills, lies

buried beneath these layers. It is composed of the same dolomite, limestone and marl. And so, in addition to the bridges and the Metro tunnel, Buda and Pest are connected by the masses of rock which form the hills of Buda and Pest beneath the river at increasing depth as they approach the latter.

Apart from being interesting from a scientific point of view, these circumstances have their practical significance as well, namely, in the exploration for thermal springs.

Budapest owes its abudance of thermal waters to the same geological fault-line which played such an important role in the development of the Danube's bed. Presumably, a series of earthquakes broke up pre-existing huge masses of rock which then slipped apart to create fissures that made it possible for immense quantities of hot water to well up without hindrance from the deep. In Buda

these emerged at the surface in the form of springs; in Pest they rose only as far as the buried dolomite layers.

Hungary is the land of thermal springs. There is hardly any part of her territory where drilling deep would fail to bring thermal water to the surface. The first explorations to this end were carried out in the 1860s. Budapest was included right from the beginning, as Buda had been famous for its natural hot springs long before. It was remembered that thermal waters had existed on the small islet which had disappeared near the northern end of Margaret Island; thus exploratory drillings were attempted on Margaret Island, too. The 44°C water that rises from a depth of 118 metres, originated from a layer of dolomite similar to that from which Buda's natural thermal springs emerged.

The next explorations were carried out in

46. *The Palatinus spa on Margaret Island*
47–48. *The Gellért and Rudas Baths receive their waters from the thermal springs on the Buda side of the Danube bank*
49. *The Lukács Baths and Pool*
50. *The Széchenyi Baths in City Park*
51. *In the medicinal waters of the Széchenyi Spa*

Városliget, the large City Park in Pest, about three kilometres from the Danube. With the rudimentary equipment of those times, the drilling took several years; finally it was successful and a thermal spring of 74° C gushed forth from a depth of almost a thousand metres, again, originating in the dolomite layer.

Since then Pest has several other thermal wells and also thermal baths fed by them. Many of Hungary's thermal springs have a curative effect, and Budapest may rightly be called a city of spas. Visitors have continued to come here primarily for the sake of their health, to take advantage of the various services offered by the thermal baths.

In praise of the hillsides

City buildings always divide space into vertical and horizontal planes. This applies to New York as it does to Budapest or Melbourne. Of course, roofs may be slanting, and various elements of buildings may have other than plane surfaces, but this will not change the priority of and emphasis upon the vertical and horizontal planes.

The human spirit finds it difficult to bear the depressing dominance of vertical and horizontal planes and the rectangular corners and angles so characteristic of large cities. The greatest achievements of architecture — in the pyramids, colonnades, porticos, vaulting, domes, apses, pagoda-roofs, as well as the innovations introduced with the Gothic and Baroque styles — all seem to have sought some sort of remedy — the resolution

of the apparent constraint imposed by a spatial order governed by gravitation — in various other solutions for breaking up the space we inhabit. The spectacle of artificial slopes formed by stairways generally creates such an effect.

But how much more does the sight of natural slopes, the natural domes of mountain peaks, or the pagoda-roof angles formed by the valleys between them, the steeply falling rocky mountainsides with peristyles formed by multitudes of living trees and the Baroque-style ornaments presented by their knotted forms and branches!

It is invaluable for a city to be rich in such natural features, and unforgivable not to

make the best use of them. We must admit that Budapest is not altogether blameless in the construction of buildings that do not harmonize sufficiently with the lines of its peaks and ridges. However, the city's location is so favourable that the greater part of its natural features have survived in spite of all the errors. This goes not only for the city's overall aspect and open perspectives, but for its details as well.

Castle Hill is somewhat more densely built up than the other hillsides, but even here a sense of liberation from the confinement of the "main planes" of the city can be felt. And this is even more the case with Gellért Hill and Sashegy.

55

56

52–57. In praise of the rows of steps

58. *At the foot of the hills: the Tabán*
59. *Statue of Bishop Gellért on Gellért Hill*
60. *Turn-of-the-century lamp-posts on the stairs leading to the statue of Bishop Gellért*
61. *The main figure of the Liberation Monument*

61

60

Gellért Hill is named after an Italian bishop, the righ-hand man of the first Christian king of Hungary, St. Stephen (1001—1038), who worked zealously for the organization of the Church and the conversion to Christianity of the Magyars. St. Stephen's statue surmounts Castle hill, that of St. Gellért the hill named after him, near the spot whence—according to legend—insurgent pagans rolled the pious bishop down into the Danube in a barrel lined with spikes.

Today, when one makes one's way down the lower gradient of the south-western slope, the soothing sight of fig trees with abudant fruit divert the spirit. It is such a surprise that one wonders how figs got there at all!

They are probably of Italian origin and most likely left their homeland even before the saintly bishop. In fact, it is presumed that they were transplanted to this cooler country by settlers coming to Pannonia from the Roman Empire.

They have been thriving here ever since,

together with the sweet chestnut trees, also of Italian origin, growing sufficiently well hereabouts as evidence that the Mediterranean climate makes itself felt even in the surroundings of Budapest.

This is due mainly to the Carpathians, which border Hungary and hinder the inrush of cold air from the north and north-east into the central Danube valley. To these likewise Budapest owes its comparatively mild winters, as well its fairly dry sunny early autumns, which last from mid September to the second

62

63

62. *The cable railway takes its passangers to the plateau just under the summit of János Hill*
63. *The Pioneer Railway winds its way along the forest-clad hills of Buda, up to Hűvösvölgy*
64. *But nothing beats treading a forest path on foot*

64

half of October, when the grapes, figs and sweet chestnuts ripen.

Once Buda also produced famous wines.

But a metropolis, Budapest today no longer needs viticulture. It is more important that the expanding city should not spread across the forest-clad slopes of the hills and areas formerly occupied by vineyards; and it is important that there should remain sufficient open country for recreation.

No complaint can be raised in respect of Gellért Hill, which has the city's most beautiful parks. The neighbouring Sashegy has not been built in, and its rocky upper part has with its rare plants and animals been declared a nature conservation area. The metropolis hums far below, but peace and quiet reign on the peaks and neighbouring hillsides.

The woodlands extending uninterrupted over many thousands of acres of undeveloped undulating country, a little further from the Danube, is an even more invaluable asset of the capital. Here the gardens of the houses and the neighbouring forest merge without effort; the city does not actually end at their

68

69

65–67. *Statuary from the late 19th century on the buildings at Nos. 9, 2, 12, Népköztársaság útja (Avenue of the People's Republic) the only true avenue of the city*
68. *Detail of the façade of the Academy of Music*
69. *Courtyard near Népköztársaság útja*
70. *Detail of the Opera House*

70

border. Well-kept walks, grounds allocated for physical exercise, benches, small wooden shelters against sudden showers await hikers in the oak forests and beach-groves. There is also the hundred-year-old cogwheel railway running its winding course some 12.5 km in length on Szabadság (Liberty) Hill; and the cable railway, operating under the name *Libegő*, takes you almost to the very top of János Hill within a few minutes.

Rationale of the City

The hills, valleys and rivers were not created by human agency, yet they have all found their proper place. Nor was special pattern of the city designed solely on the drawing boards of engineers. The gradual expansion of settlements has its own laws, and Budapest is no exception. The main sections of the capital's two nuclei, Pest and Buda, developed along the two banks of the Danube. The people who settled needed adequate protection such as defensible stone walls could provide.
It is worth tracing the remains of these walls.

43

71. *Along the Avenue each house has its own character (No. 90 Avenue of the People's Republic)*
72. *The Avenue ends at Heroes' Square*

Parts of the present existing boulevard—in Buda, Mártírok útja, in Pest, the Kiskörút (Tolbuhin körút, Múzeum körút and Tanács körút)—run roughly along their ancient lines. One might say that the old town-walls determined the line of the future inner boulevards, and the boulevards, for their part, determined the points at which the Danube bridges were built.

Afterwards, the plan of the city developed accordingly. Roads like Váci út, Majakovszkij utca, Rákóczi út and Üllői út, which spread out from Budapest towards other towns, had their origin at the respective gates

73

74

73. Heroes' Square
with the Millennial Monument
74–75. Triumphal chariots
top the Monument's pillars
76–77. The square is bounded on the left
by the Museum of Fine Arts and on the right
by the Art Gallery

in the walls. So when purposeful townplanning began in Pest, it required no special wisdom on the part of the planners to develop the already established pattern of boulevards and radiating thoroughfares. In Pest, where level ground made it possible, the course of another ring, the so-called Great Boulevard (today's Ferenc körút, József körút, Lenin körút and Szent István körút), and later on a third, were mapped out and the existing radial thoroughfares were widened.

The obvious development in the lay-out of Budapest, which took place virtually of its own accord, accounts for the irregularities in the main thoroughfares mentioned above. The boulevards do not describe a perfect arc, nor—with one exception—do the radial thoroughfares take straight courses either.

79

80

81

From the collection of
the Museum of Fine Arts:
78. *Leonardo da Vinci (1452–1519):*
Head of a Warrior (The Red Head)
79. *Raffaello Santi (1483–1520):*
Portrait of Pietro Bembo
80. *Lucas Cranach (1472–1553): Salome*
81. *Pieter Bruegel the Elder (c. 1525–1569):*
The Sermon of St. John the Baptist
82. *Gustave Courbet (1819–77): Wrestlers*

82

There is one exception which is a true avenue, the work of town-planning engineers of the last century. It was actually built the way they conceived, planned and created it. They wanted it to look the way it is.

The thoroughfare we refer to is as straight as the crow flies. It is wide. It is spacious. It is flanked by rows of trees and villas. In a single decisive leap it joins the most densely populated nucleus of the city with the beautiful open spaces of the City Park. Its original name was Sugárút (The Avenue). Now it is called Népköztársaság útja (Avenue of the People's Republic).

The thoroughfare was criticized at the time for leading to the park. Why make the city's main thoroughfare run into a park? And why close it, even before it reaches its destination, with the large expense of Heroes' Square? But when looking at the pattern—and beauty —of the city as a whole, one has to admit that the broad thoroughfare has contributed a great deal to it. The mere fact that it broke up the crowded quarters of Pest was an important improvement; at the same time, it created a worthy setting for some fine public buildings, amongst them the Budapest Opera House built very much in the style of the Vienna Opera. Furthermore, it enabled the town-planners to develop on the fringe of City Park the most beautiful square in Pest, Hősök tere (Heroes' Square). Last but not least, it brought the Park itself closer to the heart of the city, especially after the subway —the first electric underground railway in Europe—was completed.

83. *El Greco (1541–1614): Mary Magdalene*
84. *Francisco Jose de Goya (1746–1828): Portrait of the Wife of Juan Augustin Bermudez*
85. *Angelica Kauffmann (1741–1807): Portrait of a Lady*
86. *Camille Pissarro (1831–1903): Pont Neuf*
87. *Pablo Picasso (1881–1973): Mother and Child*

88–89. *Vajdahunyad Castle,*
the pride of City Park
90. *The lake of City Park with the "Castle"*

90

91. *The statue of Anonymus,*
chronicler of King Béla III
92. *The car of the first underground in Europe*
in the Underground Railway Museum, Deák
Square
93–94. *In the winter, the boating lake of*
City Park is turned into an ice-skating ring
95. *The Széchenyi Bath*
96. *A green island in the heart of the city*
97–99. *The Zoo*

93

91

92

94

However, let us stop for a minute at Heroes' Square, if but for the sake of the millenial monument whose centre column is surmounted by Archangel Gabriel guarding the greatest figures of Hungary's thousand-year-old history. In front of the column, in the centre of the square, is the memorial to the heroes who fell for their country. On the right and left, closing the square, are two huge colonnaded buildings: the Museum of Fine Arts, housing a rich collection of Egyptian, Greek-Roman and European works of art, and the Art Gallery, the main exhibition hall for temporary shows of contemporary artists. Behind the arcaded colonnade of the millen-

95

96

97

98

99

nial monument there is an open space. The surface of City Park Lake flashes before one's eyes, with the fortress-like museum of Vajdahunyad Castle on its shore. Behind it are the vast expanses of the City Park, with the adjacent Zoo and Amusement Park.

The whole complex appears to justify the planners, the men who dreamt of and realized a more perfect order for the city.

The "Inner City" of Pest

Buda has several centres, but none of them can be called an "inner city," just as the residential quarters in its surrounding hills cannot be called "garden suburbs".

On the left bank, however, the old nucleus of the city along the Danube—the Pest section between Margaret Bridge and Liberty Bridge —has preserved its status of an "inner city" to this day.

Here one finds the best—and most expensive —restaurants and cafés, as well as the best shops. There is no match in the rest of Pest for the row of hotels along the inner city section of the Danube bank. The principal administrative centre of the country, the Parliament, is also situated nearby. As a build-

100. *The Forum Hotel*
on the bank of the Danube
101. *Café terrace in Kígyó Street...*
102. *...and a restaurant on the Danube corso*
103–107. *Open and closed spaces*
in the Inner City
108 *The row of hotels by the Danube*

103

106

107

104

105

ing, it is a monumental mausoleum of the historic illusions of the former, long vanished and scattered Hungarian ruling classes. It is crowned with a multitude of spirelets, with a dome in the middle, and constitutes the largest single building complex on the river bank. In spite of this, its neo-Gothic structure makes it appear graceful. It is an apt symbol of the illusory world of the turn of the century, when it was fondly imagined that the greatness and power of the medieval Hungarian kingdom would survive the second millennium.

The Parliament turned out to be sumptous, if somewhat showy; but people got used to it and learned to live with it. "Since it turned out as it did, nothing can be done about it. We shall accept is as our own."

The fact that the huge building complex does not dwarf any of the valuable historic buildings or monuments of the Inner City helps us excuse the Parliament its excesses. It cannot adversely affect its surroundings for its bulk is not wedged between other buildings. On one side it fronts the Danube, on the other the spacious Kossuth Lajos Square, named after the great leader of the Hungarian War of Independence. The two wings of the building are also surrounded by large open spaces.

The nearby (Liberty) Szabadság Square is also worthy of attention. Various Ministries, the National Bank, the Chamber of Commerce, the Television Centre, constitute a whole series of important public buildings.

The Inner City is studded with others, including the Hungarian Academy of Sciences, the Budapest Town Hall, the fine neo-classical building of the council of Pest County (i.e. the territory surrounding the capital), most Ministries, foreign trade companies and banks, and international airline companies; indeed, no other centre in the country is of similar importance.

109. *View of Parliament from Buda...*
110. *...and from Pest...*
111–112. *In part, and in whole*

However, even in this feverishly active centre, there are refuges for quiet contemplation. The centuries-old palace of Count Károlyi's family houses the Museum of Hungarian Literature, named after the 19th century revolutionary poet, Sándor Petőfi. One of the interesting buildings in Kossuth Square is the seat of the former Supreme Court which now houses the Ethnographical Museum. The romantic-style Vigadó or Redoute, now the Municipal Concert Hall, of which only a few smouldering ruins survived the devastation of the war, but

113

114

115

113. *The Gallery of Parliament*
114. *The grand staircase*
115. *The sixteen-pointed stars of the cupola*
116. *In a quiet corridor, statues recall the past*
117. *The Assembly Hall*

118–123. *Old statues in the Inner City*

122

MAGYAR TUDOMÁNYOS AKADÉMIA

123

which has since been fully restored—is the scene of concerts, recitals and fine arts exhibitions.

Some of the churches of the Inner City also deserve mention. The oldest one stands on the river bank, at the Elizabeth Bridge. Part of its foundations are Roman ruins, part of its structure is built over its own remains, for the first version dating from Roman times was destroyed by Mongolian invaders in 1241–1242; later, the church was reconstructed in the Gothic style. Still later, Renaissance chancels were added to it, and during the period following, its façade was restored in the Baroque style. These historically different items fit together well. The only thing that may stick out is the small Turkish prayer-house attached to the southern wall of the chancel. It is indeed unusual in a Roman Catholic

63

124. *Romanticism and functionality (Vigadó Square)*
125. *The garden of the former Károlyi Mansion*
126. *The two Virgin Maries of Martinelli Square*
127–128. *Underpasses help speed traffic at Felszabadulás (Liberation) Square*

129–133. *Felszabadulás Square and vicinity in the heart of the Inner City*
132. *Panorama of Pest from Gellért Hill*

church; yet it is not surprising if we bear in mind that for a century and a half (1541–1686) the church was used as a Mohammedan mosque.

The Baroque churches of the city also delight the eye. The finest among them are the University Church and the Franciscan Church. There are also two Greek Orthodox churches of interest, one Serbian and one Hungarian. Finally, in the Inner City stands St. Stephen's Basilica, the largest church in Hungary, named after the country's first Christian king. It was built in the mid-nineteenth century after several starts, because the dome collapsed while under construction. The front elevation of the huge building faces a relatively small square, but in spite of this it offers a fine view with the simple inscription above its doorway: EGO SUM VIA VERITAS ET VITA.

131

133

132

134. *Roman ruins near the Danube bank of Pest with the Inner City Parish Church in the background*
135. *Portal of the Catholic Church in Váci Street*
136–137. *University Church, one of the best examples of Baroque architecture in Pest*
138. *The Basilica*

Where is Budapest?

Where exactly is Budapest, you may ask. One answer is: between Vienna and Belgrade. Its geographical co-ordinates are indicated by every map as latitude 47° 30′ north, and longitude 19° east. The same parallel passes through the city as goes through Bregenz in Austria, Winterthur in Switzerland, Angers in France and the north-western city of Seattle in the USA; and the same meridian as through Tromsö in Norway, Gungun in Zaire and Worcester in South Africa.

Still, these data tell us little about Budapest, except that it is situated a little nearer to the North Pole than to the equator, and that the clocks run on Central European time, which means that they are one hour ahead of GMT. However these positional aspects reveal little

of the city's geographical and historical situation which so influenced its development. It will help to convey a clearer picture if we say that Budapest is one of the metropolises of East-Central Europe. It belongs to Central Europe, however, even if situated in its eastern part.

For us, today, Central Europe appears to have become overshadowed. The East-West political division of the Continent makes many people forget that the existence of Central Europe as such is a thousand-year-old fact of history.

This is confirmed also by Budapest. From its history, we may learn of the past of a city first founded within the Roman Empire, in the province known as Pannonia, before the birth of Christ, of a past which in the Middle Ages tied the fate of the city to that of Rome

140

141

139

142

139. *Ruins of a Roman amphitheatre in Óbuda*
140–142. *Gothic stone cornice . . .*
Turkish cupola . . . Baroque patron saint of the city, in stone
143, 146. *Neo-Classical façade of*
the former County Hall and the turul *bird of the Castle, a product of Neo Romanticism at the time of the Millennium*
144, 145, 147. *The Rococo in Buda, Eclecticism and Art Nouveau in Pest*

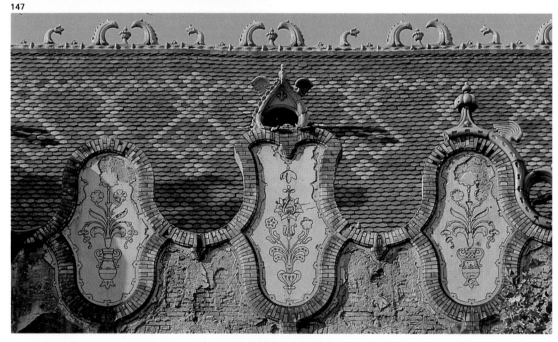

rather than Byzantium, of a past which did not seal off Hungary from the well-springs of the Roman, Gothic and Renaissance spirit and art. True, the century and a half of Turkish rule (1541—1686) caused a considerable break in its development, and the wars connected with the occupation destroyed much of what had previously been created here by the spirit and art of the West. However, some of the surviving Turkish remains add here and there special colour to the city. The eighteenth- and nineteenth-century buildings reveal the prevalence of Western influence with the Baroque, Rococco and Louis XVI styles and the later local versions of Neo-Classical and Romantic art. Hungary, and in particular Pest-Buda, were never excluded from any new or important trend in Europe, even *Sezession,* the special Austrian and Eastern

European version of Art Nouveau, or the "pure formalism" of the architecture which followed.

Ruins along the limes

From Asia Minor to Britain, the Roman Empire left quantities of ruins behind. In Budapest the remains of the ancient border defences, the *limes* of Pest, are clearly discernible even today.

It is evident that the *limes* was not a kind of ancient Maginot Line dug in the earth and filled with defensive engines. The borders of the Empire were defended by a long chain of watch-towers, forts and military camps. They were connected with each other, as well as with the back areas, by excellent roads.

Most of the permanent military camps lived

their own lives as individual settlements, often in symbiosis with the civilian towns established next to them. This is how it was in Óbuda, the northern part of present-day Buda. The twin towns of Aquincum lived together but never fully merged into each other. They even had their separate circus shows. The inhabitants of the military camp had an amphitheatre accommodating 14,000 people, while the civilian population went to another seating about 6,000. The upper tiers of what remained of these amphitheatres were carried off piecemeal by later house-builders; but the lower tiers and underground chambers which housed the wild beasts, actors and gladiators, can still be seen.

The guarding of the Pannonian *limes* was fortunately greatly facilitated by the Danube. However, to protect the crossing points on both sides of the river, the Romans built scattered fortifications on the left bank as well. This is how Transaquincum and later Contra-Aquincum became established in the second century, A. D. Ruins of later fortifications have been excavated next to the Elizabeth Bridge in Pest.

There are naturally many more archaeolgical remains on the Buda side of the river. The most extensive excavations have been carried

151
152
153

out on the site of the civilian town of Aquincum. In a garden setting with ancient ruins are to be seen the remains of dwelling houses, baths, shops and shrines, as well as a market hall and carved wells. The most remarkable exhibit in the Aquincum Museum is a 52-pipe water organ. Most of its bronze parts were found intact, so it was an easy matter to reconstruct the instrument.

Many a grave and grave-stone were also found in Aquincum. The archaeologists also encountered a trefoil-shaped old Christian graveyard chapel known as the *cella trichora,* while several Mithraic shrines proclaim widespread veneration of the Old-Persian Sun

god, which must have been introduced by soldiers sent here from Syria.

In the military town, a public bath with several pools, a steam room and central heating system remained comparatively intact. The waters of the thermal springs of Buda were also conducted to this bath.

The inhabitants of Aquincum bathed at the small island formerly situated at the upper end of Margaret Island, where abundant natural thermal springs gushed forth. However, the Danube gradually washed away the island, carrying with it the ruins of the Roman baths as well.

148. *The Roman ruins of Aquincum, former headquarters of Lower Pannonia*
149. *Roman mosaic in Buda (Meggyfa Street)*
150–152. *Finds from the Roman Empire in the Open-Air Museum of Aquincum*
153. *Roman capital among the prefabricated apartment houses of Óbuda*
154. *The gentle, southern slope of Castle Hill seen from Gellért Hill*

155

157

156

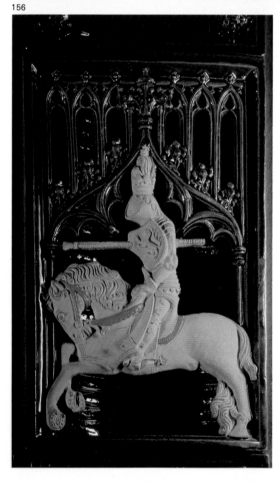

An underground kingdom

Cities do not move about, at least not in space. Perhaps in time. But time also changes the space surrounding them. Transferred political boundaries and economic lines of force may easily change their destiny.

At the time of the fall of the Western Roman Empire in the fifth century, the mid-Danube *limes* ceased to exist. So did the urban life of the region. Only a heap of ruins remained on the site of one-time Aquincum. Huns, Goths, Avars and other mounted warrior peoples of the East brought their herds to graze this side of and beyond the Danube.

A decisive change took place around the year A. D. 1000, when our ancestors, the Magyars, who settled in the Carpathian Basin, were converted—at almost the same time as the Bohemians and Poles—to Christianity, and these three Roman Catholic kingdoms established east of Germany entered on a course of European development. Soon urbanization commenced all over the Continent, giving rise to Óbuda in place of Aquincum, while Pest gradually developed on the opposite bank of the Danube. Not much later

159

158

160

Buda also began to grow as the southern neighbour of Óbuda.

At the end of the Middle Ages, these three cities formed the centre of a feudal Hungarian state extending throughout the Carpathian Basin, only to find themselves again in a peripherial position when the conquering Turkish Empire incorporated them—overnight, as it were—as European border cities of a small province under military government, with the Pasha of Buda at its head.

The Turkish occupation and the final siege, launched by united European armies to drive the Turks out in 1686, reduced the splendid medieval Hungarian royal palaces to mere ruins.

Yet, visitors to Buda Castle can project themselves into the past centuries when Buda was still ruled by Hungarian kings.

Having annexed Hungary to their empire, the Habsburgs replaced the destroyed medieval palace in Buda with a castle. This eighteenth and nineteenth-century building, incorporating parts of the ancient castle walls and bastions, had to be reconstructed again after the Second World War. From the Castle as it stands today, long flights of steps lead down

161. *Reconstructed medieval fortifications on the southern side of Castle Hill*
162. *Towers of the Lihegő Gate and the Great Southern Bastion*
163. *Bastion of Veli Bey with the memorial to the Transylvanian Hussar Regiment of the First World War*
164. *Part of the western Castle wall*

to halls and vaults of medieval origin. Numerous relics of the long-vanished medieval rous relics of the long-vanished medieval Hungarian kingdom are preserved here, most notably survivals—even if in ruins or fragments—from the palaces which once stood on this site.

In the large Gothic hall dating from around 1420 and the similarly-styled Gothic undercroft can be seen special medieval art treasures: a series of stone statues of kings, knights, ladies, and saints. According to all available evidence, they were carved in the time of Sigismund of Luxembourg, King of Hungary and Holy Roman Emperor (1387–1437). They were probably buried underground as superfluous rubbish some time in the mid-fifteenth century. Many of them were found smashed to pieces, but those which remained intact or whose fragments could be successfully assembled—after the excavation of this cemetery of sculpture in 1974—powerfully evoke the European atmosphere of nearly six-hundred years ago.

Stone carvings of somewhat later date, recalling the splendour of the Renaissance palace of Matthias Corvinus (1458–1490), are also worthy of attention. Most of them are of

165. *Silver gilt flask of Matthias Corvinus (c. 1443–1490)*
166. *White marble Renaissance portrait of Queen Beatrice (1457–1508)*
167. *Pedestal of the gold Matthias Calvary*

Hungarian red marble; but the relief carved in 1489 representing the royal couple is of Italian white marble.

Writing about King Matthias, Antonio Bonfini, the Italian humanist author said:

"On the front overlooking the Danube, he [the King] had a chapel built. This he provided with a water-organ and a double font made of marble and silver. Higher up he had a library built which he filled with a rich collection of books, sumptuous even in their covers. South from this, there is a vaulted hall, the ceiling of which shows the whole firmament... There are some spacious dining halls and superb bed-chambers. The door-frames are embellished with marquetry. The decorative fire-places are surmounted by quadrigas and other Roman-style ornaments. Below is the treasury with other store-rooms and an armoury."

And so he continues with his description. However, not long after the Turkish invasion all of this was destroyed. Part of it was buried underground, other parts still deeper, in oblivion.

170

169

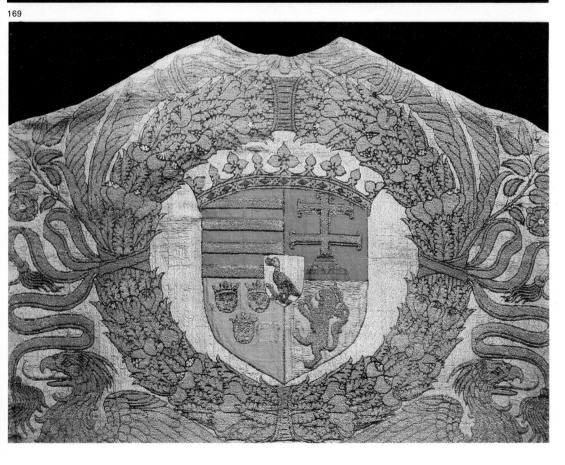

The burghers of Buda

Wherever imperial or royal castles were built on hill-tops in Europe, towns for burghers were generally established at their foot.

Castle Hill in Buda was, however, large enough to be shared by both the court and the civil inhabitants of the town.

The Royal Castle complex was naturally somewhat more spread out than the ordinary houses which are situated close to each other to this day. However, the streets of the town were never so narrow that the drivers of carriages proceeding in opposite directions or rumbling past each other would have come into collision.

The old inhabitants of the houses in Buda generally engaged in some farming, in addition to pursuing their chosen trade. They gathered in the harvest from their vineyards on the surrounding hills, just as they cropped the hay required for their animals.

Carts with their loads had plenty of room under the archways of the houses. In the side-walls of the narrow archways were rows

172. *The Mace Tower*
173–175. *Gates in the Castle District*
176. *Gothic sedilia behind the portal at No. 32 Úri Street*

of so-called *sedilia,* whose purpose has not been clarified to this day.

Many of the *sedilia* are still extant, mainly because far fewer houses were buried during the Turkish conquest than were royal buildings. Most of them were left damaged but not completely ruined after the expulsion of the Turks. Part of the walls were still standing and their strong foundations also survived. The restorers made use of these, incorporating the ruins into their new Baroque style houses.

The *sedilia* and Gothic windows were walled in, of course. The devastation of the Second World War was responsible for revealing from under the fallen plaster fragments of medieval Buda.

177. *The National Archives at the northern end of the Castle District*
178. *Statue of Pallas Athene with the coat of arms of Buda on the corner of the former Town Hall of Buda*
179. *"Floating" female figure of a Classicist appartment house on the corner of Ország-ház Street and Peter-mann bíró Street*
180. *Bay window of the former Town Hall of Buda*
181. *Where Táncsics Mihály Street runs into Bécsi Kapu Square*

Often these fragments were of considerable dimensions. There are a number of houses on Castle Hill which freed from their later extensions, plaster cornices and mortar surfaces, have regained, either fully or partly, their fourteenth-, fifteenth- and sixteenth-century form in the course of restorations following the Second World War.

The restorations involved a tremendous amount of work, for in 1945 the Castle District lay in ruins. It had already suffered earlier devastation under the Turks, as a result of which it lost its original aspect. So experts tried to restore every house in its original ancient form, though only in so far as they could follow surviving architectural elements. They always observed the strict requirements of authenticity, relying not on imagination but information gathered from the walls and stones wherever possible. They uncovered every part of the ancient houses down to the last cornerstone, and their subsequent work was determined by their findings. Thus the Castle District was reborn. It became—in spite of the previous devastation—even more "ancient" and beautiful than it had been before the Second World War.

The Gothic and Renaissance past of the district has acquired greater emphasis, as did the medieval and Turkish elements of the fortifications. Yet this emphasis is not out of proportion, and does not disrupt the basically Baroque atmosphere of the Castle District.

Sometimes, the late evening hour or a summer night seems to conjure up the ancient aspect of Buda in the minds of people stroll-

182. *Fortuna Street and Táncsics Mihály Street begin at Bécsi Kapu Square*
183. *Old gate in Országház Street*
184. *Bay-window of the house at No. 5 Bécsi Kapu Square*
185. *Houses on Fortuna Street*
186. *Early Neo-Classic apartment houses on Bécsi Kapu Square*
187. *Window on Bécsi Kapu Square*

188

189

191

192

190

193

ing along its streets. Let us cite here Gyula Krúdy, the great Hungarian Impressionist writer of the beginning of the century, who wrote in one of his novels:

"Mr. Rezeda lived in Buda in the Castle District; walking home at night, he often met kings who stepped out of the stone walls. Rezeda politely lifted his hat before Matthias, who wore a student's gown, or before the grim figure of black-bearded Sigismund; he would remain standing beside the bastion with head bent until the phantoms of the kings—composed of the mist of autumnal nights, the silver of the pale moon, and dully echoing ringing of bells

90

194

195

188–193. *Façade and corner decorations on the old houses of the Castle District*
194. *Baroque fresco on the façade at No. 16 Táncsics Mihály Street*
195. *Façade of the house No. 10 in Táncsics Mihály Street*
196. *Café in Fortuna Street*
197. *Medieval commercial building with characteristic second level which juts out at No. 14 Tárnok Street*

196

197

198–202. *Gates and yards at No. 16*
Táncsics Mihály Street, No. 25
Fortuna Street, at No. 16
Országház Street and No. 31 Úri Street

200

201

198

199

202

in ancient towers—disappeared again some-
where along the Castle walls. On other occa-
sions he stopped in one of the deeply slumbering
streets to listen to the sounds of revelry that he
fancied came from underground, from cellars
and vaulted tunnels under the Castle. Who
knows which king's brave warriors had been
left behind in the cellars under the Castle be-
cause of their drinking bouts. . .? Then, ladies
of the Court, enveloped in cloaks, stole past
him in the silent night with steps as noiseless as
the wind in a grareyard. Some of them had
golden heels on their little shoes. The wings of
their cloaks touched Mr. Rezeda's shoulders" . . .

Such fantasies, however, require the dead of
night. Kings? Soldiers? Ladies? In day-time,

203–204. *Wrought iron flag holder and old gate in Fortuna Street*
205. *Row of windows at No. 16 Táncsics Mihály Street*
206. *Old dwelling houses in Táncsics Mihály Street*

205

203

204

206

it is the recollection of substantial tradesmen and craftsmen that best suits the streets, mews, archways and courtyards, whether they date back two, four or five hundred years.

The ancient citizens were Germans, Hungarians and Jews. The latter lived in what is today's Táncsics Mihály utca, called Jew Street at that time. To posterity they left two medieval synagogues and some ancient tombstones. Excavated Jewish relics are at present in a special small museum.

The Germans and Hungarians had their separate churches. The German one, originally called the Church of Our Lady, is at present known as the Matthias Church. Under Turkish rule it was converted into a great

207

209. *Baroque coat of arms on the façade of a mansion at No. 58 in Úri Street*
210–211. *Old maple-wood gate of the same mansion*
212. *The former Town Hall of Buda on Szentháromság Square*

209

210

211

208

207. *Medieval carved stone cornice at No. 20 Országház Street*
208. *Fortuna Street*

94

213. *The famous Ruszwurm Confectionery in Szentháromság Street*
214. *One of the towers of the Matthias Church*
215. *Baroque and Neo-Gothic: the Trinity Statue and Matthias Church*
216. *A new statue and building on Szentháromság Square*
217. *Matthias Church seen from the park below Fishermen's Bastion*

214

215

213

216

mosque or *djami;* later it was restored in Baroque style; only at the end of the past century did it regain, through repeated restoration, if not exactly an identical, yet a very similar appearance to the original Gothic building. There was also a Hungarian Church dedicated to Mary Magdalene, which was likewise reconstructed in the Baroque style. Visitors to the Castle may find some recompense for this loss in the Gothic remains incorporated in the Hilton Hotel complex, some of them only recently uncovered. Something quite unusual happened in this connection in the 1970s. The modern hotel was built in the immediate vicinity of Matthias Church, on a site where previously the remains of a medieval Dominican monastery dedicated to

218

219

220

218–220. *Matthias Church*
221. *The sanctuary*
222. *The southern gate*
223. *Sitting figure of King Matthias built in the side wall of the medieval Nicholas Tower*
224. *The Hilton, built behind Baroque walls*
225. *The espresso terrace of the Hilton*

222

221

223

St. Nicholas stood, together with the monastic church and a later Baroque building. The new building construction not only spared all the historic remains but organically attached them to the hotel. Open-air concerts today are held within the walls of the ruined church; the former cloisters, with an original carved stone fountain, were incorporated into the hotel premises. The Baroque building also serves the hotel's purposes, as does the medieval tower next to it, the western wall of which shows the seated figure of King Matthias. This carved stone relief is an authentic copy of the contemporary work produced in Bautzen (Silesia).

The word "copy" may have a disillusioning

224

225

effect on the visitor. However, it is better not to deceive ourselves. It must be borne in mind that the followers of Mahomet did not tolerate the representation of the human form in their country, except on miniatures. Matthias himself had an original fifteenth-century statue in Buda which, however, showed a standing figure, not a seated one. The King had it cast in metal, similar to the statue of his father, János Hunyadi, whose victory in 1456 against the Turks at Nándorfehérvár (now Belgrade) is commemorated by the ringing of church bells at noon all over the world. The King had a further statue cast of his brother László, whom the young and jealous Habsburg ruler, Ladislas V, beheaded only a few months after the triumph at Belgrade, which had saved the country from Turkish invasion. All this belongs to the past, and it was a matter of course that it had to perish when Buda became Budin, a border town and jealously guarded stronghold, an advanced base of the Turkish Empire in Europe.

226. *Neo-Romanesque towers and terraces of the Fishermen's Bastion*
227. *The Bastion with the statue of St. Stephen*
228. *One of the staircases of the Bastion*

228

229. *Turkish "turbaned" tombstones on the side of Castle Hill*
230. *Memorial plaque to Kassim Pasha on the wall of the bastion he had built*
231. *Turkish cupolas of the Király Baths in Watertown*

The Crescent Moon over the town

The Turks of today hardly understand why their ancestors evoke so many bad memories in Hungary. They like the Hungarians, and always have. They harboured the Hungarian freedom-fighters Thököly, Rákóczi, Kossuth together with their followers, protecting them against the Habsburgs. Thus they sincerely deplore when—of all nationalities—Hungarians consider them barbarians, devastators and enemies who ruined their country. Sultan Suleiman II and his successors did not come to Hungary to lay waste the land. They came to conquer in the name of the Prophet, under the green flag of Allah, to win or to die. Hungary was destined to be the scene of a hundred- and- fifty years of war between the great Islamic Empire of the Turks and Christian Europe. Here ran the front-line, moving back and forth. It was here that enemies had to cause as much damage as they could, not only to a country's forces but also to her castles, towns and villages. It was regarded heroic not merely to defeat but to weaken the other: to burn, devastate and plunder on the other side of the front. And of course, to kill, murder and even drive away the surviving inhabitants.

According to certain historians, the whole period of Turkish rule did not damage Hungary as much as the war of liberation in the 1680s. In 1686, after a siege lasting several months, the Castle of Buda fell to the united Christian armies as a mere heap of ruins. The town was also in ruins, as was the former Royal Palace, that is to say, the historic buildings of Hungary, as well as those dating from

Turkish times. Of the latter, only some bastions survive here and there.

For the record, let us add that of the twelve *djamis* in Buda, one actually survived the siege of 1686 and one stood in Pest for some time after that date. Religious intolerance was evidently responsible for their later disappearance. It was not during the war, but in the peaceful eighteenth century, that they vanished.

Fortunately, bathing was not a thing prohibited by the Christian faith, even though it did not enjoin it as strictly as Islam. Thanks to this the pickaxe spared four beautiful baths built or reconstructed in the Turkish style in Buda in the second half of the sixteenth century. They still stand at the foot of Castle Hill, not far from the Danube. Two of them, the Király and Rudas baths, lend the city an Oriental character with their typical domes composed of spherical segments reminiscent of Turkish *djamis*. The other two, the Császár and Rácz, in use to this day, also preserved their dome-shaped roofs.

Another similar building with a characteristic dome recalling Turkish times in Buda is the *türbe* or funeral chapel of the dervish Gül Baba which stands on the Hill of Roses (Rózsadomb) north of Castle Hill. The crescent moon of the followers of the true faith of the Moslems glitters on its top even today.

Peace times, German times

After the expulsion of the Turks, a century and a half of peace descended on Pest-Buda, or shall we say Pest-Ofen. The latter name was more befitting in an age when the major-

ity of the inhabitants of both cities were German. Even the third community, Óbuda, or Alt-Ofen as it was known then, was occupied by them after the end of Turkish rule, when the Habsburg emperors residing in Vienna extended their power beyond Hungary, over the whole of the Carpathian Basin.

The emperors gave strict orders that only Germans, and Roman Catholic Germans at that, should be permitted to settle in the occupied towns.

Since the first half of the sixteenth century there were many Protestants—Lutherans and Calvinists—among the Hungarians. The number of "rebels", just as reluctant to bow to the Viennese Emperor as they had been to cringe before the Sultan of Istanbul, was considerable.

So settlers came to Buda, Óbuda and Pest and other Hungarian cities from the German Em-

232. *The Szarvas (Stag) House at the southern foot of Castle Hill*

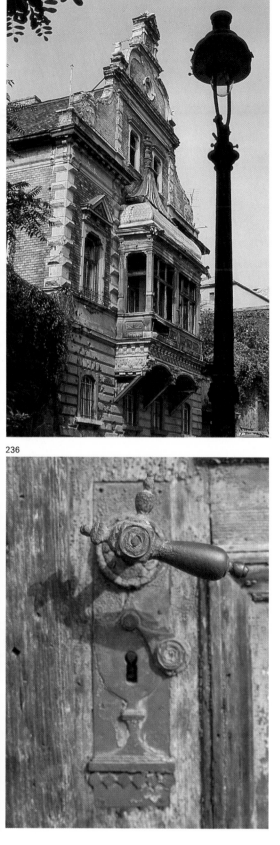

pire. They were a mixed crowd of honest, decent tradesmen and craftsmen, but there were among them rather dubious elements as well.

The latter were numerous. In the newly established towns, the prisons were crammed; it took some time before the better-class of immigrants prevailed over the criminals and adventurers.

However, the buildings dating from these times show no trace of the chaos that reigned in the city, only that after lengthy struggle a period of lasting peace gradually set in. It was also a period of material growth, the building of the three cities on the Danube and the destruction of the Turkish *djamis* with their domes and slender minarets.

The style of the age was Baroque. It came to Hungary, too, although it did not reach the

233–234. *Houses in Ostrom Street, on the northern side of Castle Hill*
235. *Old house in Hunfalvy Street,*
236. *Old iron door-handle*
237. *The Lajos fountain on Corvin Square*
238. *Baroque statue of St. John of Nepomuk on the façade of the house No. 3 on Corvin Square*

territories under Turkish rule. Once the Turks had been driven out, the field was open to all ranks of masters of Baroque architecture. They left their mark on a large number of buildings both in Pest and Buda.

There were Italian and Hungarian architects among them; but most came from German territories. The effect was fruitful, just as fruitful as the Romanesque, Gothic or Renaissance styles had been at the times they became naturalized in architecture in Hungary.

The result was no doubt due partly to the large masses of German settlers, those who commissioned and those who executed the buildings.

Let us grant them their due! But at the same time, let us reject the contention that the backward barbarian Hungarians would not have been up to the task of creating an urban culture of any value without the help of the German settlers.

The kingdom, the power and the glory belonged to Vienna at that time. It was the Vienna of that period which decreed that the Hungarian citizenry was not to be allowed to grow too strong, least of all the citizens of the heart of the country, the two towns of Buda and Pest. In the eyes of the Hungarians, Vienna meant the Imperial Court. The Emperors there reigned over the land of Hungary as kings; but they neglected to make Budapest even their secondary seat, such as Prague became. For a long time, even the Royal Council of the Governor-General did not have its headquarters in Buda but in a western border town of Hungary, Pozsony (now Bratislava). Pest and Buda became provincial towns and life pro-

239–242. *St. Anne Church on
Batthyány Square, one of
the most beautiful Baroque monuments in Buda*
243. *The old terrace of the building on
the corner of Fő and Pala Streets*
244. *Louis XVI style window in Szalag Street*
245. *Down in the distance Watertown,
towards the sky, the Castle*
246. *The Rococo building of the former
White Cross Inn on Batthyány Square*

ceeded there accordingly, far from Vienna, bathed in the brilliant light of imperial splendour.

However, a century later the offices of the Hungarian authorities moved to Buda. Certain restrictions had already been relaxed earlier: Hungarians had the right to settle, buy or build a house in Pest-Buda. Nevertheless, it took a long time before they outnumbered the Germans and a Hungarian Budapest was finally born.

Still, almost all the eighteenth century Baro-

247

248

249–250

247. *Statue of Eugene of Savoy (1663–1736) in front of the main façade of the Castle*
248. *Northern gate of the Castle's inner courtyard*
249. *The high cupola*
250. *The western wing is the new home of the National Library*
251. *A view of the inner courtyard*
252. *Ornamental fountain in front of the façade facing the Danube*
253–254. *The eastern wing of the Castle houses the National Gallery. The gallery of the cupola and the grand staircase*

que houses recall the early German small towns of Pest, Ofen and Alt-Ofen. The same applies to the Baroque churches and other contemporary buildings. The statue dedicated to the Holy Trinity, standing on Szentháromság Square in the heart of the Castle District, was also destined to protect the pious German population of the town against the raging plague of the time.

It was around this period that the building of the new Royal Palace was began. Not a single surviving wing of the ruined palace was

251

252

254

From the collection of
the Hungarian National Gallery:
255. *Master of the St. Anne Altars
(early 16th century): St. Anna Altar from
Kisszeben (detail)*

256. *Master of Jánosrét (15th century):
Main Altar of Jánosrét (detail)*
257. *Hungarian painter (15th century):
The Madonna of Bártfa*

255

256

257

spared. The devastation caused by the Turks and the siege was completed by the pickaxe: King Matthias's once famous palace was literally razed to the ground. The stones and rubble were than levelled and the foundations of the new royal residence were built over them.

The new building was not planned to be either too large or too sumptuous, for the Habsburg rulers had not the slightest intention of moving from Vienna to Buda or even of spending a long period of time there.

When the palace was finished, the first wing was still very modest. Two further wings built in the Viennese Baroque style were added by Maria Theresa (1740–1780). The Baroque remained the dominant style also for the large-scale extension of the residence in the nineteenth century. However, no trace of it is extant today. After the siege of the Second World War, the huge building was restored in a much more puritan form. It now houses the National Széchényi Library, the Hungarian National Gallery, the Budapest Historical Museum, and other important cultural institutions.

A country in search of a heart

Vienna had never been accepted by Hungary as her "heart", for she never wanted to merge into the Habsburg Empire. Hungary wanted a destiny and a heart of her own. There was in this attitude a good deal of close-fistedness on the part of the Hungarian nobility. That of Austria and Bohemia had long lost its fiscal immunity, while Hungary still stood upon her ancient constitution and laws. In view of these circumstances, Maria Theresa decided to regulate the customs duties in a way that would make Hungary a safe market for Austrian and Bohemian industry and a steady supplier of cheap food and raw materials. Speaking of Hungary and Transylvania, one of her counsellors openly declared that he regarded these countries in the same light as the Indian colonies.

Prince Metternich, the great nineteenth century politician, was of the same opinion. "Hungary needs no industry," he declared, "every poor man there is needed for agricultural work."

However, the effects of this policy did not spare the German population either. It even made part of the Hungarian nobility partisans of civic progress in the country.

And so, the aggrieved parties found each other. Hungary began to feel that she did have a heart. It no longer mattered so much

258
258. Mihály Munkácsy (1844–1900):
Condemned Cell
259. József Rippl-Rónai (1861–1927):
Woman with Cage

260. Lajos Gulácsy (1882–1932):
The Magician's Garden
261. Béla Kondor (1931–1972): *Christ I*

261

259

260

262

that the German settlers outnumbered the Hungarians in Pest-Buda.

From the first decades of the 1800s, common endeavours became more and more marked. The nobility gradually realized that their close-fisted policy was not profitable. It was not worth while to be the privileged class of a backward country, the poor seigneurs of miserable serfs. General and proportionate sharing in taxation, freely flowing credit, free-ly circulating money, a developing industry, modern agriculture, the people of an independent country living and working for their own good, became the dominant aspirations of Hungary.

This exciting age left its mark on external aspects of the city as well. The features of Budapest—especially Pest—first of all on those of its building which were conceived in the Neo-Classical style.

Thus far, Buda had been in the lead over Pest. After all, it was there that the great kings of old had their seats, and the Turkish pashas ruled. The new Royal Palace of the Habsburgs was also built in Buda.

In the first half of the nineteenth century, however, Pest was being built up and generally developed. Trade on the Danube became more lively; the western provinces of the Em-

112

pire needed increasing quantities of Hungarian wheat, wine, wool, leather and other agricultural products which could be most conveniently transported over water. Due to the Napoleonic wars, oats and hay were also in great demand. The centre of exports of these from Hungary was Pest, and goods imported in exchange were also delivered here. The launching of public projects encouraged

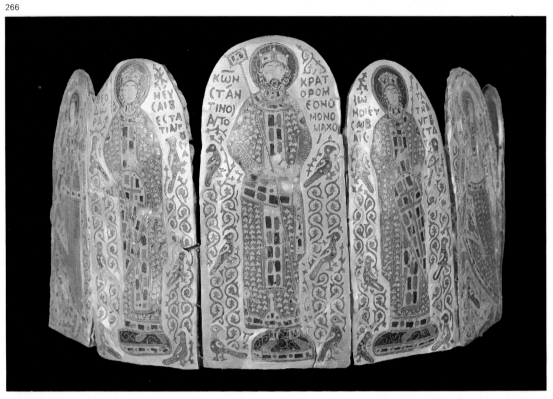

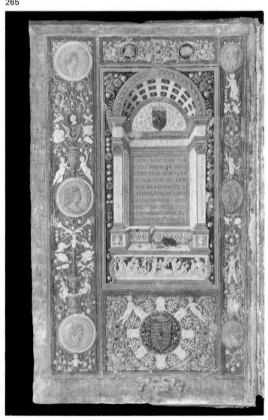

From the collection of the National Museum:
264. *Scythian golden stag, 6th century B.C.*
265. *Title page of an illuminated manuscript from the Bibliotheca Corviniana*
266. *The Monomachos crown, 11th century*
267. *Lehel's horn, 9–10th century*
268. *Crown of St. Stephen, 11th century*
269. *Ornamental cup with lid, 1697*
270. *Miklós Barabás (1810–1898): Laying the Foundation Stone of the Chain Bridge*

wealthy middle-class citizens to invest their money. Three and four-storey houses and business establishments sprang up along the Danube and elsewhere within the city walls. In Buda, on the other hand, there was hardly any private building activity; it remained the small Baroque town it had been before, while Pest gradually grew into a large city dominated by the then fashionable Neo-Classical style.

Traces of these developments are still evident in Budapest, although hardly any of the Neo-Classical buildings of the age stand out conspicuously among the later eclectic ones.

One of the finest Neo-Classical historic monuments of the city is the edifice of the Hungarian National Museum with its flight of steps, colonnade and tympanum. It is a worthy spokesman for its times, the embodiment of respect for the past and hope for the future. It was built by the sons of a nation already aware of the fact that it was worth while to build a lasting home for the preservation of the country's historical relics and other public treasures.

There was never any uncertainty about the site of the building. It had to be erected in the heart of the country and in Pest, the city pervaded by the breath of the new times.

Yet nobody suspected then that this beautiful new building was soon to become the scene of historic events. Nobody knew that from the base of the huge new columns, on the steps of the Museum, resounding revolutionary words would arouse the assembled masses on the morning of March 15, 1848, when Sándor Petőfi's famous poem "Talpra magyar" (Rise, Hungarians) first incited the nation to rebellion.

The movement for national revival, already many decades old, turned into a true revolution. The long period of slow, prudent progress was followed by one of radical reforms, rapid changes in society and eventually armed struggle for the independence of the country, lead by Lajos Kossuth. It was a

popular-national struggle and only the joint forces of two great powers—imperial Austria and czarist Russia—succeeded in suppressing it in blood in the late summer of 1849.

Years of labour

"The mind was aflame and the heart filled with hope." Hardly any other words could characterize better or more concisely the period preceding 1848. They were written by Mihály Vörösmarty who, after the defeat of the 1848–49 Hungarian War of Independence against the Habsburgs, became a persecuted refugee.

Pest and Buda, although not reduced to ashes, suffered a great deal from the cannons and siege during the war.

It looked then as if the country had no hope.

The saying: *"finis Hungariae"* was no longer just a bad nightmare. The victorious powers divided Hungary into separate regions with local centres, all of which were controlled directly from Vienna.

Pest-Buda again ceased to be the heart of the country. But such complete numbness and hopelessness could not last long. Life did not come to an end. Industrious craftsmen continued their work, tradesmen their trade. At the beginning of 1848 the Hungarian nobility liberated their serfs, abolished their own exemption from taxation, and of their own accord introduced a general sharing of the public burdens. These measures survived the defeat of the revolution and proved favourable for the development of the bourgeoisie. This applied especially to Pest, which soon availed itself of the advantages of rail trans-

272

273

271

274

276

port in addition to the shipping on the Danube. Where money circulates, people cease to brood over the past. Not only tombstones were set up; houses were built too.

The architecture of the age was characterized by the late-Romantic style. The buildings then created were all individualistic. Most important were the Hungarian Academy of Sciences, the Vigadó (Municipal Concert Hall) where Liszt and Brahms gave recitals, and the Synagogue of Pest in Dohány utca. The latter points to the increasing role played by the Jews in Hungary's economic life. The revolution of 1848 achieved for them a comparative equality of rights and the possibility of free enterprise. They had a stake in preserving Pest-Buda as the heart of the country even when it did not exist officially. These were no easy times. Tears mingled with blood while they lasted. However, in 1867, after long procrastination, Francis Joseph and the liberal Hungarian politicians came to a compromise. Long-drawn-out negotiations resulted in the birth of a dual monarchy, two co-dominions with equal rights and separate parliaments; two reponsible governments but one Francis Joseph who, although he continued to act as Emperor in Vienna, was only regarded as King of Hungary by the population of Budapest.

The birth of a metropolis

In the ancient coat of arms of the Habsburg dynasty, a double-eagle spreads its black wings. In 1867, the Habsburg Empire also became double-headed, with one head in Vienna, the other in Budapest.

Vienna had grown into a large city a long time before; but in comparison, Budapest was still somewhat undeveloped. It was time to catch up with Vienna, not only in size, but also in beauty, not just in the number of stones, but also in the quality of cultural life. Modern town-planning began. Boulevards and avenues were built. Strict building regulations directed development into the desired channels. A city-wide water-, sewage- and gas-system were developed, and public lighting and solid pavements formed part of the new projects. Bridges were constructed over the Danube. The city was enriched with new theatres and an Academy of Music that rivalled the one in Vienna; an Opera House, picture galleries, museums, exhibition halls and a Polytechnic were also built. The huge Parliament Building, the Stock Exchange and a series of other public buildings were among the newly erected establishments.

European architecture was dominated by the Eclectic style. This meant a practically unlimited mixture of styles, a little of this, and a little of that. The buildings of the age showed a combination of details that would hitherto have been regarded as incongruous. Romanesque, Gothic, Renaissance, Baroque, Neo-Classical and even romanticized elements appeared side by side. Now one was emphasized, now an other, often with the ostentatiousness of the newly rich.

Indeed, the greater part of Budapest was at that time the city of the newly rich. The members of the thriving bourgeoisie—whether of German, Jewish or some other origin—proved to be enthusiastic Hungarian patriots. Equality of rank for Hungary within the Habsburg monarchy was propitious in no small way for the Hungarian capitalist investors. This applied to the whole country, but in particular to Budapest. The rapidly developing railway network converging on Budapest brought most raw materials here for processing, and excess rural manpower was also absorbed by the capital. On the outskirts of the city and even within its boundaries a

278–279. Newly painted Eclectic mansions along the Great Boulevard and Museum Boulevard

280

280. *The silent statues of the Basilica and the bustling city*
282–283. *Bajcsy-Zsilinszky Road: Eclecticism and Art Nouveau*
281., 284. *Two gates and two styles on Szent István Boulevard*

282

283

284

281

variety of new factories were built, accompa-
nied by overcrowded apartment houses for
the workers flocking to Budapest. This had,
above all, an animating effect on inner Budapest which grew in size as well as in wealth.
The beauty of the eclectic apartment houses
masked as palaces has since worn off. Good
style in architecture mellows with age; what
is merely showy later causes disappointment.
The question arises as to what happens when
such buildings get restored, repainted or re-
juvenated in some other way?
In Pest—which is a truly eclectic city—there
have recently been attempts to do this by
giving some of the main thoroughfares a face-
lift. The experiment was not without success.
The freshly painted houses have lost their
hundred-year-old tiresomely dull aspect and
—as if by some miracle—have become res-

122

285

286

287

285. *Rooftops of the Inner City*
286. *Szent István Boulevard*
287. *19th-century ornamentation on a façade*

123

plendent again. The question remains: for how long?

It is evident, however, that the values that the Eclectic buildings represent in Pest, the beauty that in the great palace-like apartment houses have been preserved, are worthy of consideration, the more so because the public buildings of the city followed this style from the building of Parliament to the Opera House, from the Cathedral to the Budapest Library, from the Neo-Romanesque Fishermen's Bastion to the Neo-Romanesque-Neo-Gothic-Neo-Renaissance-Neo-Baroque building complex in City Park.

But is it beautiful? Let the question go unchallenged. It is interesting, no doubt about that; as interesting as the whole of one-time Budapest which vied with Vienna and developed feverishly in its striving to become a real metropolis.

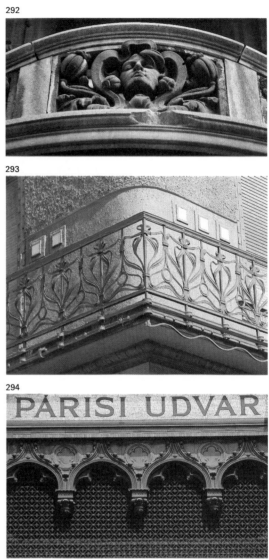

292

293

294

The troubled beginning of the new century

At the end of the last century the city grew and developed rapidly, but not restlessly. Then, a certain strange restlessness set in. There was something in the air that made itself felt not only in Budapest, but throughout Europe. Was it the smell of gunpowder? The premonitory sign of a cruel war, or of an all subverting revolution? Nobody reckoned with a cataclysm like the one that affected the world in 1914, though people did expect some menacing change.

At the beginning of the century, the Hungarian capital was already one of the important centres of the artistic endeavours which arose from this restless, foreboding outlook. It is perhaps sufficient to mention the names of Csontváry, the painter, Béla Bartók and

295. *The Art Noveau period between the two world wars in architecture: what is not functional can't be beautiful (Houses on Madách Square)*

295

296. *The blending of the centuries in Óbuda*

.

Zoltán Kodály, the composers, György Lukács, the philosopher, and Endre Ady, the poet.

Budapest had no architect of such stature. But it did have some who were capable of perpetuating in their buildings the restless modern spirit, the negation of past, and the search for new ways of expression which prevailed here in the early part of the century. They were the architects who created the Hungarian version of the European Art Nouveau.

They were extreme individualists, like all artists who followed this new trend in the arts. So they never developed a common style. Yet their works embodied the same spirit of the age; an age that no longer knew whether it could believe in itself, and this very doubt made it bold. Its boldness developed under the pressure of circumstance. It was mocked and even held in contempt by modern architecture, though the latter only took wing before the First World War and gained ground repeatedly after it. We now hold it again in higher esteem, and do not believe in discarding everything that architecture has achieved by a rejection of earlier combinations of colours, lines, planes and space.

Between the two world wars

At the end of the First World War the Habsburg monarchy collapsed. The states of the Carpathian Basin, including thousand-year-old historic Hungary, fell to pieces. Since 1867, Budapest had been the capital of the eastern half of a European Great Power, the centre of a territory of 300 thousand square kilometres. Of this, only 93,000 remained.

Vienna suffered the same fate. But neither city diminished in size on that account. On the contrary, they became comparatively larger. In such cases the law according to which disproportionately large cities absorb everything, concentrating in themselves all the energy destined to promote development, is fulfilled. Being already too large, cities continue to grow, although this is no longer good for them.

Half of the country's industry was concentrated in Budapest and its surroundings. First one-sixth, later one-fifth of the population came to live here. Among all the European countries, only Austria had such a disproportionately large capital at that time. The much talked of predominance of Paris over the provincial towns of France did not even approach the relationship of Budapest

or Vienna to the provincial communities of their respective countries.

Budapest is just as centrally situated as Paris; it forms the junction of a star-shaped road and railroad network. No excuses were offered; the Hungarian capital had to develop further. It had to swell, grow, become built up, even if at a slower pace than before, and even at the cost of leaving other parts of the country comparatively undeveloped.

By this time the architects cursed Art Nouveau. Rational, simple, yet aesthetic three-dimensional forms were now being adopted in Budapest. Elements devoid of func-

tion were barely tolerated, on the grounds that what is not functional cannot be beautiful.

Although a new style set in, it left few marks on the architecture of the 1920s and 30s. This was partly due to the impoverished state of the country. Moreover, the years of construction were very soon followed by the devastation of yet another war.

The present and the future

After the Second World War most of Budapest lay in ruins. However, the 1944–45 devastation of the city did more than merely cause distress, it raised hopes, too. For it was to be followed by the advent of a great new epoch. The people of Budapest, liberated at last from Hitlerian domination believed and hoped that all the old evils could be made good. All they had to do was to bury the past and accept the promise of a better future.

All at once, everything was in ferment. Daring new ideas were born in the field of

town-planning. Outstanding architects thought the time ripe, for instance, for opening green corridors in the densely built districts of Pest, to allow open passage to the fresh air flowing almost continuously from the forests of the Danube Bend. However, this dream soon vanished when the housing shortage caused the shelving of every such town-planning idea.

For obvious reasons, only those houses were demolished after the war which had been so severely damaged as to be absolutely uninhabitable and whose restoration was quite hopeless. Even so, the streets were studded with vacant lots. Gradually most of these were built up. To link such lots into a green corridor would have required the sacrificing of whole blocks of crowded town dwellings, and the moving of the people living in them elsewhere. But where?

This "where" has remained a vital problem up to the present day. In the meantime, the demolition of damaged older houses has become ever more urgent in the densely built inner districts of Pest. People crammed into the "belly" of the city have a craving for more space, larger grassy expanses, more trees, air and sunlight.

In the past decades, new housing estates have increased the number of dwellings in Budapest by hundreds of thousands; yet even so, shortages still exist. True, some of the housing estates necessitated first making a clean sweep of existing old buildings. In Óbuda, for example, whole rows of old one-story houses had to be levelled.

On the outskirts it was easy to demolish structures, but in the inner part of Pest it is still impossible, even today.

This may, however, be a fortunate circumstance. The decades of delay brought about something good; for besides the further aging and decay of the century-old public housing units, there has grown up an ever increasing attachment to *historic* Pest.

The antique stones of Buda carry with them a 700-year-old history, while the ruins of Óbuda have a history of nearly two millenia. Pest can boast no such antiquity. It lacks, above all, anything similar to the Castle District blessed with so many ancient remains rising above the more recently developed parts of the city.

Apart from a number of scattered Baroque, Neo-Classical and Romanticized buildings, inner Pest is dominated first of all by the Eclectic and Art Nouveau that has survived from the turn of the century. This gives it a

297–299. *It would be a shame to destroy everything that is worn or old...*

300

300–303. *The too rational lines of the new buildings only enhance our nostalgia for the more personal beauty of bygone times*

303

301

302

historic atmosphere, and as the years go by, will make the city even more interesting and valuable, especially in the face of the growing number of bleak panel houses in the new housing estates.

It is clear by now that the Inner City on the left bank of the Danube must be renovated and opened up with all due consideration to its heritage. While green areas must be provided, the notable creations of modern architecture, together with the whole pre-First World War aspect of the city, that "newly rich" inner part of Pest which grew so eagerly in the old days, must be revived and preserved.

On the old outskirts, most of which became attached to Budapest in 1949, the situation is different. In these areas there are hardly any remains worth preserving, and architects can have a free hand. They must bring the housing projects to a successful conclusion, building flats by the thousands and ten thousands, as well as stores, libraries, schools, sports grounds and others establishments without which a modern housing estate cannot exist. Historic Pest and Buda remain the main centres of the capital. It is proposed, however, to make the surrounding sub-centres grow as attractively as possible, particularly as de-

129

306

305

veloping cultural centres. For it must be born in mind that new homes may facilitate, but cannot in themselves bring to fullness the lives of people in the multi-storied standardized buildings of the new housing estates. It is imperative that they be less dull, less monotonous. Today, everyone is painfully aware of the rapidly rising demand for just this.

The town-planners of Budapest must also reckon with this demand. A rational order of forms and colours is important. Important, yes, but not sufficient. Man is not only a rational being. He also has a soul, sentiments, attachments and a constant desire for something new. That this has been recognized, appears from the articulated forms and lively colours of schools in the new housing estates. There are many individually designed buildings, generally surrounded by carefully tended parks. The urge towards the humanizing of the environment also shows up in the many new statues, monuments and fountains set up in public squares, and even in the growing appreciation for historic districts and especially for Art Nouveau decoration.

The inhabitants of the city

Who live in Budapest?
Many kinds of people throng the main streets and thoroughfares of the city. One hears different languages spoken. However, those speaking a language other than Hungarian are almost certain to be tourists, businessmen, specialists, reporters, delegates, foreign students studying in Budapest, etc.—People who happen to be here now but will leave soon.

Almost all those who settle here come from different regions of Hungary. They make up for the lack of increase in the population which typifies most large cities.

In most economically-advanced countries, the only reason why the population of big cities does not diminish rapidly is because there are continuous replacements coming from smaller settlements. This applies also to Budapest.

A few decades ago, there were so many people moving into the capital that the number of its inhabitants grew rapidly. It reached and even exceeded the two million figure; but then the increase stopped, and more recently, a slow decrease has set in. As it is well known, this is always incidental to a certain process of ageing. But for the time being, this hardly shows in the life of the city. Whichever part of the world people come from, when they are

314

confronted by the day-to-day life of Pest and Buda, they see that this Central European metropolis is inhabited by a very energetic people.

This is, of course, partly due to the fact that Budapest, with its two million inhabitants, attracts almost every important organization to itself from the whole of Hungary. Here we find the largest scientific institutions, research centres, libraries, archives, museums, theatres and orchestras; the only Hungarian film studios, the national radio and television headquarters; it is here that the most outstanding artists and writers work, most university and college students study; ministries and other national institutions function along with industrial and trading enterprises, banks, and insurance companies. All this gives the city an advantage over others within the country, and contributes to its undisputed dynamism. But Budapest owes its vitality also to the openness without which no small country can hold its own any longer in the world. Although its main virtue lies in the fact that it is the queen of Hungarian cities; its inhabitants are well aware that this superiority is but relative, that they must watch the people in other countries, learn and get information from them, take part in the international exchange of material and intellectual life and in the obstinate rat race of these days, in a way that even in critical circumstances will not make Hungarians the losers.

Budapest is today one of the most sober metropolises of Europe. It aspires to neither more nor less than it is capable of. It indulges but little in fancies or reveries: instead, it perseveres in its search for realistic approaches to the future.

Budapest is neither young nor old; its situation has not predestined it for either. It may yet see difficult times, but its sources of strength are inexhaustible; as long as people continue to live here, it will always be reborn. The present-day inhabitants of Budapest soberly reckon with their circumstances. They recall the fate of two thousand-year-old Aquincum, one thousand-year-old Pest-Buda, the ruined city of the winter of 1944–1945, and they do not doubt that Budapest will always survive and find new possibilities for prospering.

Today this matter of survival and prosperity is in their own hands. They work for it, and their labour is evident on the face of the city. However, the result of earlier labours, those of their ancestors, Hungarians and non-Hungarians alike, some known by name and others unsung, are also there. These forefathers deserve our love and gratitude for what Budapest is today.

304–314. *It's not a new city, but nor is it old*

133

The photographs were taken by:

Imre Benkő	43
Lóránt Bérczi	12, 50, 140, 141, 146, 156, 172, 221, 226, 230, 252, 291
Lajos Czeizing	36, 38, 114, 116, 117, 132, 225
Sándor Cs. Kovács	277
László Csigó	17, 18, 34, 49, 50, 62, 295
Tamás Diener	25, 26, 27, 28, 76, 77, 92, 93, 102, 104, 105, 118, 187, 189, 196, 198, 203
János Eifert	95, 97, 98, 99, 103, 106, 107, 113, 115, 117, 120, 121, 124, 247, 248, 251, 254, 301, 302
István Faragó	15, 22, 65, 67, 179, 188, 197, 207, 209, 240, 283, 285, 287, 288, 289, 290, 292, 293, 294, 299, 313
Ernő Fejér	55, 192
György Gara	6, 11, 16, 24, 31, 52, 53, 56, 57, 59, 94, 139, 144, 145, 148, 161, 163, 164, 175, 176, 182, 183, 185, 191, 193, 200, 201, 202, 204, 205, 210, 211, 212, 215, 217, 218, 219, 220, 222, 233, 234, 235, 236, 237, 238, 239, 241, 242, 243, 244, 249, 250, 281, 284
László Gyarmathy	4, 41, 47, 48, 73, 138, 147, 157, 158, 271
András Hász	64, 100, 135, 136, 137, 276
György Hegedüs	312
Károly Hemző	3, 5, 20, 29, 91, 101, 109, 119, 123, 134, 162, 213, 224, 229, 231, 262, 275, 307
János Huschit	70, 282, 296
Károly Kastaly	160, 206, 300
György Kapocsy	96
Péter Kornis	7, 23, 88, 89, 90, 131, 143, 208, 246
Albert Kozák	(MTI) 155, 159, 253
Lajos Köteles	194, 199, 232
Endre Lábas	69, 133
Árpád Patyi	227
Endre Rácz	112, 142, 151, 153, 297, 298, 304
Csaba Ráffael	(MTI) Jacket, 274
Tamás Révész	35, 54, 110, 111, 228
Herbert Saphier	263
Béla Schichmann	(MTI) 154
Péter Siklós	68
József Szabó	9
Zsolt Szabóky	1, 2, 10, 13, 14, 19, 21, 32, 39, 40, 42, 44, 58, 66, 71, 74, 75, 122, 124, 126, 127, 128, 129, 130, 149, 150, 152, 171, 174, 177, 178, 180, 181, 223, 245, 272, 278, 280, 286, 305, 306, 309, 310, 311
Zoltán Szalai	273
Károly Szelényi	8, 45, 82, 125, 165, 167, 169, 170, 216, 264, 265, 266, 268, 269
János Szerencsés	37, 72, 186, 267
Alfréd Schiller	78, 79, 80, 81, 83, 84, 85, 86, 87, 255, 256, 257, 270
Gyula Tahin	63, 108, 173, 195, 279, 303
Bence Tihanyi	166, 168
András Tokaji	30, 33, 46, 51, 60, 184;
István Vidovics	314

Third edition
Design by Zoltán Kemény
Text by Domokos Varga
Translation by Elisabeth Hoch and J.E. Sollosy
© Domokos Varga, 1985
ISBN 963 13 2567 9

Printed in Hungary, 1987
Kossuth Printing House, Budapest
CO 2589-h-8789